Wait for Me

Life of Father Junipero Serra

Written by
Sister Mary Helen Wallace, FSP

Illustrated by
Denis Thien

Missionaries of the Sacred Heart
1197 Woodrow Road
Clarksburg, OH 43115
(614) 495-5653

St. Paul Books & Media

Library of Congress Cataloging-in-Publication Data

Mary Helen, Sister, FSP.
  Wait for me : the life of Father Junipero Serra / written by
  Sister Mary Helen, FSP ; illustrated by Denis Thien.
      p.   cm.
  ISBN 0-8198-8232-1
    1. Serra, Junípero, 1713-1784—Juvenile literature. 2. Explorers—
  California—Biography—Juvenile literature. 3. Explorers—Spain—
  Biography—Juvenile literature. 4. Franciscans—California—
  Biography—Juvenile literature. 5. California—History—To 1846—
  Juvenile literature. [1. Serra, Junípero, 1713-1784.
  2. Missionaries. 3. California—History—To 1846.] I. Thien,
  Denis, ill. II. Title.
  F864.S44M37 1988
  979.4'02'0924—dc19
  [B]
  [92]   88-13103
                                                                       CIP
                                                                        AC

Printed in the U.S.A., by the Daughters of St. Paul
50 St. Paul's Ave., Boston, MA 02130

The Daughters of St. Paul are an international congregation of women
religious serving the Church with the communications media.

        1 2 3 4 5 6 7 8 9 10   96 95 94 93 92 91 90 89 88

CONTENTS

CHAPTER 1

UNRAVELING THE MYSTERY

Margarita looked up as Miguel slipped through the back door and appeared in the kitchen.

"I'm home from school, Mama," he announced. Mama wiped her floured hands on her apron. She hugged the boy and smiled.

"I know what you want," Mama said. "Wouldn't a glass of milk taste good? And look...a slice of bread still warm from the oven."

"Thank you, Mama," the boy said as he made himself comfortable on the chair. While Miguel ate his snack, Mama was deep in thought. Her son was fifteen. His big eyes were full of mystery.

Miguel was short and his youthful face made him look younger than he was. The boy was a good student at the school of San Bernardino near his hometown in Petra, Spain. Miguel studied religion, reading, writing, Latin and mathematics. But the most exciting part of the school was the gray-robed friars, with their hoods and sandals. To Miguel and the other students, the Franciscans were holy men.

He loved their gentle ways, and their smiles, and the games they taught between classes. Miguel often followed one or the other of the friars with his piercing eyes and would say with conviction, "I want to be one of them."

The glass was empty; the plate was, too, but Miguel was still sitting at the table, staring straight ahead. Mama sat down. She knew her son very well.

"Would you like to talk about it?" she asked. "Or would you rather wait until Papa comes home?" Mama thought of her husband, Antonio, the village blacksmith.

"Mama, I want to become a Franciscan friar," Miguel stated flatly. His voice was earnest, eager for her approval.

"But I thought you had to be sixteen to become a novice," Mama said, trying to be as gentle as possible.

"Yes," Miguel answered, "but if you and Papa give me permission, I can attend the Franciscan school in Palma until I am old enough to become a novice."

Mama's eyes fell. Palma was twenty-five miles away from their hometown of Petra. Why, that almost seemed like the other side of the world.

"Are you sure this is what you want?" Mrs. Serra asked.

"Very sure," came the reply.

Mama nodded her head and replied quietly, "I will talk to Papa."

The donkey-drawn cart crept along the road while the sun burned without letup. It was the year 1729. Antonio and Margarita looked ahead as they were swayed by the rhythm of the cart. Miguel hummed a little tune. He was excited. Antonio guided the reins of the donkey as Mama reached over and placed her hand on his.

"Remember the day he was born, Antonio?" Her husband responded with a nod. "Remember when we took him to our Lady's shrine?" Mama asked. The blacksmith nodded again.

November 24, 1713, had been one of the happiest days of their lives. On that day, their son, Miguel Jose Serra, had been born. Later the couple had welcomed Juana Maria, Miguel's younger sister. But now Mama was caught up in the wonder of the moment.

"A gray-robed Franciscan," she said softly. "Imagine, our Miguel might become a son of Saint Francis."

"Who knows?" Papa called over the sound of the cart wheels. "If it is the Lord's will, let it be."

"Of course, we will miss him," Mama added. "In fact, we will miss him now while he will be at school. But..." she glanced sideways. There were tears in Antonio's eyes.

CHAPTER 2

THE ANSWER...

Miguel kicked the pebbles on the dusty road as he shuffled along. The sun was hot and blinding. It reflected off the white-washed buildings of Palma. Miguel squinted and raised his hand to shield his eyes. There it was, straight ahead: the *Convento* of Saint Francis. The boy knew it well. He attended school here every day.

But *this* day was different. Miguel was not coming to study. The great wooden door came closer and he walked more slowly.

"O God," he prayed, "help me to say what I must. Strengthen me!" He lifted the knocker on the door and let it fall. Within seconds, a smiling Franciscan friar appeared.

"Yes, what may we do for you?"

Miguel swallowed hard. "I'm here to see Father Provincial," he stammered.

The friar looked at the earnest young man. He hesitated only a moment, then smiled again and said, "Please come in. I will tell Father he has a visitor." In a minute he was back and beckoned for the boy to follow him. Miguel's heart beat faster.

"Padre Perillo," called the friar, "here is your guest." Then while Miguel stood outside of the room, the friar turned and strode down the long corridor, leaving the young man to speak with the priest. He knocked timidly on the partially opened door.

"You may enter," answered a voice from within.

As Miguel stepped into the room, he came face-to-face with a smiling friar sitting at a desk.

"What can I do for you, young man?" the Franciscan asked cordially.

"Father Provincial, I have come to ask for something I want more than anything else," Miguel stated with determination.

"If it is *that* important I am not sure I can give it to you, but I will do my best," answered the priest who by now was thoroughly amused.

Solemnly, the boy introduced himself. "I am Miguel Jose Serra, a student here at the *Convento*, Father. I would like your permission to join the Franciscan Order." These words seemed to bounce through the air and stun the priest.

At this point, Miguel was interrupted by the soft chuckling of Padre Perillo.

"Impossible, son!" the priest exclaimed. "Why, you're only a boy. Our rules require that no one under the age of sixteen may enter."

"Oh, but I *am* sixteen, Padre," answered Miguel. He moved closer to the desk, his dark eyes piercing the priest. "I know that I'm small but I *can* work hard and I *will* grow—I *know* I will!"

Now the friar's smile turned into a grin. "Come back in a few years, Miguel, and I promise you, we will talk about it again."

Miguel tried to say more but the words stuck in his throat. Tears stung his eyes. Quickly he turned away. Padre Perillo called after him, "I'm sorry, Miguel," but the boy was gone. Frustrated, he ran blindly through the streets of Palma. He came to a halt at the foot of the cathedral.

Slipping inside, he fell to his knees. There, in the cool stillness, he poured out his soul to the One who understood, and he begged the Lord for an answer. Why was his size such a problem? Why this unnecessary delay in following his vocation? The minutes ticked by. As Miguel prayed, the ice in his soul gently melted and he was at peace.

Miguel Jose Serra was not about to give up. He would find a way. If it were God's will that he be a Franciscan, God himself would bring that about in his own good time. What Miguel did not know was that he had not long to wait.

Just three months after his sixteenth birthday, Miguel had requested permission to enter the Order. His Franciscan teachers learned of the crushing refusal. They hastened to assure Padre Perillo that Miguel was *indeed* sixteen. They explained also that his enthusiasm would more than make up for his short stature. The friars were convincing. So, when he was almost seventeen, Miguel entered the Franciscan Order. It was September 14, 1730, the Feast of the Exaltation of the Holy Cross.

Miguel looked down at the long gray robe. He smiled and said
to himself, "I can't believe I am really here."

CHAPTER 3

A NEW NAME

Miguel looked down at the long gray robe. He adjusted the cord around his waist and fixed the hood so it laid carefully on his shoulders. He paced back and forth, practicing how to walk in sandals. The young novice smiled and said to himself, "I can't believe I am really here." Everything about his new life fascinated Miguel: daily prayer, the joy of companionship in community, the spiritual classes and household tasks.

During quiet times, Miguel delved into good books, stories of lives of saints, especially those who had been missionaries and martyrs.

As a large book lay open on his plain, hard desk one day, the novice's eyes became glued to the pages that told of the life of Francis Solano, a Franciscan hero, who had just been declared a saint.

"He was a missionary far away in South America," Miguel read. "Saint Francis Solano labored with all his strength to bring the gospel message to the Indians." The image of the new saint seemed to rise right out of the pages of Miguel's book.

"Come, come and imitate me," Solano challenged. "Reach out to those who have so much less than you. Give them your love and your compassion. Share with them your gift of faith, your love for Jesus." The novice slowly closed the book.

"I want to be a missionary," he said firmly. "Yes, I want to be a missionary like you, Saint Francis Solano."

Finally, the wonderful day came when Miguel gave himself entirely to God: the day of his religious profession. He had learned that members of religious orders take vows of poverty, chastity and obedience as a sign of love for God. These special promises bind a person closer to God. For the rest of his life, he talked about that *great day* and exclaimed, "All good things came to me together with my religious profession. I even gained health and strength and grew to medium size. I credit all this to my profession for which I give infinite thanks to God."

On the day religious profess their vows, some of them select a new name, usually that of a saint whom they can imitate. Miguel chose the name *Junipero*, after one of the early followers of Saint Francis. The first *Junipero* was remembered for his humility and good-natured disposition. Miguel wanted to be just like him. Now he would no longer be Miguel Jose, but Fray* Junipero.

---

*The title given to a priest or brother who has professed religious vows in the Franciscan Order.

Six years passed by, years in which Junipero studied theology and philosophy. Then he was ordained a priest and was assigned to be a teacher. Father Serra's students loved him. With admiration, they watched the gentle priest. Two of those students, Francisco Palou and Juan Crespi, were especially impressed by him. They would be his good friends, and he theirs, for the rest of their lives.

Six years passed by, years in which Junipero studied theology and philosophy. Then he was ordained a priest.

CHAPTER 4

A DREAM TO LIVE AND SHARE

Father Serra's lips were turned up in the faint trace of a smile. He had a secret desire locked in his heart. Why did he look out among the rows of his gray-robed students and imagine Saint Francis Solano to be among them? Why did he seem to see the same saint peering amid the papers he graded and the books he used to prepare for classes?

"The Indians are waiting for you," Junipero heard in his heart. "They are waiting for you, Junipero, for the sound of your voice, for the impression of your sandals on the rough dirt trails."

The priest laid down his books and stared up at the crucifix on the wall of his bare room. His dark eyes were fixed on the cross as he asked, "Lord, how can my dream become a reality?"

One day, word came that Franciscan missionaries were needed far away in New Spain, present-day Mexico. Junipero's heart pounded. Was God inviting him to go? He would have to pray over it, but in the meantime, he asked for advice and

permission to apply. Soon there was a rumor buzzing among the Franciscans that someone from
their province intended to answer the call for missionaries. No one really seemed to know who it
was, though, and the *last* person to be expected
was the brilliant scholar and professor, Father
Serra.

One day Francisco Palou, now a priest, was
working at the desk in his room amid stacks of
books and papers. Concentration had been diffi-
cult lately because his mind kept turning to distant
lands...New Spain, to be exact. He, too, wanted to
be a missionary. Finally, the interior struggle became too much. Should he apply or not? He set
aside his books. It was time to seek some good
advice from Father Serra.

Just as Francisco Palou pushed back his chair
and stood up, a knock sounded at his door.

"Come in," answered the young friar. The
door opened and Palou flashed a wide smile.

"Junipero! I was just about to come and see
you. I have something I *must* ask you about. I need
your advice."

His eyes met the steady gaze of his friend's.
He paused a moment and then blurted, "I have
heard that someone from our province plans to
volunteer to go as a missionary to New Spain. I,
too, want to go to teach the Indians about the true
God, whom they do not yet know. Of course, I am
young...." His eyes were shining with determination. "I don't have any experience, Father, but I

truly feel that God has chosen me for this mission. Of course...," he added with hesitation, "if it is not part of his plan, he will show me the path to follow through the advice of my superiors."

There was a moment of stunned silence. Overcome with emotion, Junipero turned away. Father Palou rushed to the side of his friend.

"I'm sorry, Junipero. How could I have been so thoughtless?"

Father Serra wheeled around, his joy plainly evident through the tears that streamed down his cheeks.

"Oh, Francisco, *I* am the friar who desires to go to the New World. As sorrowful as I was in making this great journey alone, I would have set out all the same. But I decided to make two novenas to ask God, if it be his will, to give me a companion. God has given you the same desire. It must be his will, but let us entrust our intention to him and not speak of it to anyone for now."

Quickly, the two priests put in an application for work in the foreign missions, only to find that the quota had already been filled with thirty-three friars from Andalusia, Spain. There would be no room on this voyage for Serra and Palou, but the friar in charge promised to keep them in mind. It was a disappointment, but as usual, Junipero put everything in the hands of God and waited patiently.

CHAPTER 5

THE LONGEST "WAIT"

Palm Sunday morning of 1749, Father Palou was on his way to bless the palms at the church. Suddenly, a messenger came up to him, breathing heavily.

"Father," he gasped, "here is a very important letter for you from Father Mezquia."

Francisco Palou opened the envelope eagerly. His hands trembled. What was the message? His eyes fell on the clear, large words and a frown crossed his face.

"Why have you and Father Serra not yet appeared in Cadiz?" asked Father Mezquia in the letter. Cadiz was the harbor city where a group of Franciscans were already gathered, waiting to sail to the New World. "Why the delay when such an urgent request for more missionaries has already been sent?"

Palou continued to stare at the letter. He had heard nothing of a request for more friars.... Perhaps the first letter had been lost. Now, however, his superior would have to be made aware of the summons—and as soon as possible!

Francisco Palou opened the envelope eagerly.
His hands trembled.

"I can hardly believe it," the young priest said, half out loud, half to himself. Joy flooded Father Palou's soul. His face flushed. Suddenly, Junipero's words echoed in his memory: "Trust in the holy will of God. He always rewards our confidence one way or another."

Then with a smile, Francisco Palou was off down the road. He met with Father Superior who gave his permission for the two brave priests of his province to answer God's call to be missionaries. Junipero did not yet know. Father Palou's footsteps were light and quick as he made his way to Petra to tell the good news to Father Serra.

"I couldn't believe it, Junipero," exclaimed Palou. "Five of the friars who were supposed to make the voyage were frightened off at Cadiz. The ocean's high waves made them fear the long sea voyage. Then, of course, you and I were first on Father Mezquia's list of substitutes, and look...."

Father Palou's smile filled the room as he dangled the letter in front of Junipero and said, "Oh, how wonderful!"

Father Serra laughed heartily. "Francisco," he stammered, "you are so excited that I can hardly make out your words." Then he smiled and his kind voice spoke his feelings. "I really do understand, Francisco. God has been so good to us—*too* good. We must do all we can to repay his infinite generosity."

CHAPTER 6

THE HEART'S CRY

Antonio and Margarita Serra could not have been happier on that Easter Tuesday of 1749. Banners waved as a joyful procession of the citizens of Petra climbed the hill on pilgrimage to the shrine of their Madonna.

Seventy-three-year-old Antonio moved one foot ahead of the other as he prayed, "Mother Mary, bless our fields. Give us an abundant harvest."

Margarita, two years younger, joined in singing the hymns honoring the Madonna and clung to Junipero's arm. She was so proud of him. Juana Maria rejoiced in her parents' happiness.

Fray Junipero prayed and sang all the way up the hill. When the pilgrims reached the top, the songs and prayers ceased. Father Serra looked down at the scene below. He let his gaze slowly span Majorca, the island of his birth. He saw the fields, simple houses, and the blue Mediterranean Sea. His own town of Petra looked small and so peaceful.

The Serra family spent time in the beautiful shrine of Mary at the top of the hill. For Junipero, the whole day was unique and precious. Time seemed to stand still as his family sat down to eat the lamb pies Mama had made for the occasion.

Outwardly, Junipero was his usual serene and gentle self. Inwardly, he was offering to his Lord one of the greatest sacrifices of his life. Father Serra knew something that his family did not yet know. Soon he would board a ship to sail across the Atlantic Ocean. The New World awaited him.

Junipero would never again see the dark, loving eyes of his mother, or hold her close, or see the look of satisfaction on her face when her son, the priest, walked into a room. He would never hear his father's hearty laugh, or see those gnarled hands that had fed and clothed the family. He would no longer feel his father's firm, playful slap on the back. And the delicate face and thoughtful ways of his sister, Juana Maria, were soon to become just a memory.

The priest's heart seemed to break as he ate the delicious, homemade lunch. He could not tell them now. He *would not* tell them and ruin a joyful day that would live on in all of their memories. Instead, he would write to his beloved family before boarding the ship in Cadiz.

Father Serra kissed each one tenderly and returned to Palma, where twenty years before, he had joined the Franciscan Order. The wonderful memories of Petra and Palma would be with him for the rest of his life.

April 13 would be departure day for Fathers Serra and Palou, the day they would leave the island of Majorca, never to return. That day came soon enough and found Father Serra giving a last look around his cell in Palma. Yes, everything was ready. He stood for a moment and gazed out the window. Now it was really *good-bye* to Palma and Petra.

Junipero and his friend, Francisco, were willing to leave all they treasured on this earth to go far away and preach the Gospel to those who still had not heard about Jesus.

CHAPTER 7

NO TURNING BACK

Junipero stood on deck, looking out over the water as gray waves pounded against the ship. The priest's cape blew violently in the wind. He wrapped it tightly around himself. His small frame seemed dwarfed by the sea.

A rough, deep voice thrust him back to reality.

"Priest!" a man called angrily. Junipero spun around. The Captain came forward, staggering slightly, partly from drink, partly from the rocking of the boat.

"Priest!" the man said again. The word tasted terrible to him. He spit it out as if it were snake venom.

"See this book, priest?" the Captain asked, waving his large Bible. "We're going to talk religion, my little man." He edged closer to the Franciscan and pressed him to the rail of the ship. The Captain's eyes lit with wicked glee. He set down his Bible and flashed a knife. Slowly, he lifted the knife until the sharp, shining point touched Junipero's throat.

Father Serra's face remained serene. He felt the cold steel against his skin and held his breath. He stared hard at the Captain. The Captain stared back.

Time seemed to stop. Junipero prayed in his heart. The Captain scowled. For some reason, he pulled the knife away and slid it back into his belt. He cursed as he pushed the priest aside. He picked up his Bible and strode angrily off the deck. Junipero hurried to the small room where his friend was sleeping.

"Francisco," he exclaimed, "this is no time to sleep! Perhaps tonight we will receive the gold and silver crown of martyrdom." Francisco opened one eye, then the other. He listened as Junipero explained what had happened. He decided he wasn't too enthusiastic about receiving the crown so soon.

The two priests spent a restless night. The boat docked safely the next morning. Junipero and Francisco had arrived at the first stage of the journey, Cadiz, Spain, on May 7, 1749. They found that there was still room on the ship, *Nuestra Senora de Guadalupe,* for three more priests. Father Junipero sent word to three Franciscan professors who had asked him to remember them when there was again a need for missionaries. Their names were Fathers Verger, Vicens and Crespi. Father Crespi had been one of Junipero's students at the University.

There in Cadiz, the thought of his elderly parents came forcefully to Junipero.

"I have to write and tell them about my decision to be a missionary to New Spain," he said to himself. "By now they must know, but I couldn't say it before. The words were not there."

The priest wrote: "...You remember, my dear Father, many years ago, when, having received the last sacraments, you believed yourself close to appearing before God? I recall your words as if you had just spoken them; and with them I remember the promise I made to you, as you asked me then: 'Always be a good son of Saint Francis.' Very well, then. It is to carry out your will, which is also God's will, that I am now on the way to Mexico.

"My dear Mother, I know that this is what you, too, have always asked of God for me in your prayers. He has answered them already, in setting me upon the path on which I have entered. Be happy then, beloved Mother, and when you suffer, say again, with your son, 'Blessed be God! May his holy will be done.'"

Junipero set down the pen and watched as the ink dried. He stared at the words, then closed his eyes and leaned his head back. For a moment it seemed as if he could almost touch the faces of his mother and father.

Suddenly, footsteps in the corridor broke his concentration. "Is that you, Francisco?" Junipero called.

"Yes, it is," came the reply. Father Palou stepped in and walked over to his friend.

"We're ready to leave now, Junipero."

Father Serra folded up the letter, slipped it into the envelope and sealed it.

"So am I, Francisco," he murmured. "So am I."

From Cadiz, the ship, *Villasota*, sailed across the Atlantic to the island of Puerto Rico. During the weeks and months on the sea, the water supply began to run short. A sailor on board, used to the rigors of the sea, gave some of his own ration of water to Junipero and Francisco. They would never forget him.

From San Juan, the *Villasota* set sail again. A few days before arriving at Vera Cruz, a hurricane lashed the ship. The sky was black. Driven by strong winds, huge waves crashed over the deck. The Franciscans decided to write on slips of paper the names of different saints. They would choose one name by lots and that saint would be their special protector during the fearful storm. The name chosen was Saint Barbara. The priests began to pray to her, asking her to intercede before the Lord to deliver them safely. The wind died down. The waves pulled back from the ship's deck and the sea became calm. Gentle winds sped the ship to its destination.

The *Villasota* dropped anchor at Vera Cruz,
Mexico. It was December 6, 1749. The entire
journey had taken ninety-nine days. But the priests
still had one last lap to make. Their goal was
Mexico City.

The *Villasota* dropped anchor at Vera Cruz, Mexico.
It was December 6, 1749.

CHAPTER 8

WALKING ON
THE KING'S HIGHWAY

Junipero was thinking about Saint Francis of Assisi who always traveled on foot. Of course, times had changed. Several centuries had passed. Now there were ships and horses and mules available, not only for the wealthy, but even for poor missionaries. The two hundred and forty mile journey from Vera Cruz to Mexico City could have been made by ship or by land. While the majority of the friars went by sea, Junipero and another friar chose the land route.

The road was little more than a path. It continued its way from the Gulf of Mexico at Vera Cruz to Mexico City. In the other direction, the road stretched out a thousand miles from Sante Fe into Central America. The crossing point was Mexico City, Serra's destination. Somehow the dirt road had acquired an elegant name: *El Camino Real* or *The King's Highway*.

The two gray-clad friars plodded along the highway. They brought no food or extra clothing.

Their heavy habits clung to their flesh as they crawled through a jungle. The hot, muggy air circled them and seemed to choke the air from their lungs.

The friars had begun their walk on December 15, 1749. They would reach Mexico City on January 1, 1750.

One night, toward the end of the journey, Junipero felt a sharp, seering pain in his leg. The pain was followed by itching. The priest stretched out on the damp ground and the flat earth was as inviting as a feather bed. The day had been long and the journey hard. Sleep came almost immediately. While he was asleep, Junipero scratched the bite on his leg. He awoke the next morning to find that his leg and foot were twice their normal size.

Junipero looked at his red, throbbing foot and groaned softly. Silently, he prayed that the swelling would just go away. As the two friars began the new day's journey, Father Serra's companion noticed Junipero's painful limp.

"Father Serra, what's wrong? What's the matter with your leg?"

"Oh, nothing, my son," the friar answered. "Nothing that could ever slow us down, anyway."

"Father Serra, please sit down right there," said the friar firmly, pointing to a large, flat rock by the side of the trail. "Now let me see that leg," he insisted. The priest gasped as Junipero unveiled the swollen leg. "Why, you can't keep going like that! You'll never make it!"

Junipero looked at the swollen limb and nodded his head. His leg had just about given up, but his faith hadn't. Now God would have to get the wounded friar to Mexico City.

Resting when necessary, the two weary men continued on. They finally reached the Franciscan college of San Fernando in Mexico City. It was New Year's Day, 1750. They were greeted warmly by all the friars, and especially by Junipero's friend, Father Palou.

CHAPTER 9

A CALL IN HIS HEART

It was a city of striking contrasts, a city of glitter and poverty. Gold decorated the necks of some people and gaping, festering wounds marked others. All through the day and all through the night, the music of Mexico City seeped into the quiet of San Fernando College. Junipero listened. The sounds of the world did not lure him. He wanted with all his heart to grow closer to God and to bring many others with him. He began to think that it might not be so easy a task in Mexico City where, for some, God did not seem all that important.

While Junipero Serra prayed, rested and read good books, his swollen leg healed. Slowly his strength returned. The priest sensed that he would not be staying long in the city of song, laughter and dancing. He heard in his heart a call to the frontier. Perhaps it was Saint Francis Solano poking at his conscience again.

The friars were all together one evening for recreation. Father Velasco, the superior, asked for volunteers for the Sierra Gorda. He had to replace four priests who had recently died. The rough territory he spoke of was nestled in the heart of the jagged mountain range called the Sierra Madre.

"Who will go?"

"I will," Junipero answered quickly.

"And I," answered his friend, Palou.

———————————

Eight friars were chosen. Among them were Fathers Serra and Palou. While the other six priests were assigned to various regions, these two men traveled the long hard road to the Sierra Gorda. It was the year 1750. The region was hot and barren. The laughing, shimmering music of Mexico City never reached there. The only music was the buzzing of mosquitos. In fact, clusters of mosquitos and fleas followed the friars. Their sandaled feet were bitten and Junipero's troublesome leg began to swell again. The priest was glad that his long habit hid the swollen leg from his friend.

The two priests were exhausted when they arrived at the village assigned to them—Jalpan. They gazed at the adobe and thatched roofs of the church and mission. The burning sun made the friars squint.

Where were all the Pame Indians who would be their new flock? They were there in the caves and crevices of the Sierra Madre. Dark eyes watched the priests as they walked inside the crude church. Slowly, the Indians came closer to meet the Padres. Of all the baptized Indians, very few were practicing the faith.

Fathers Serra and Palou began to learn the Pame language from the Indians. Eventually, Junipero was able to translate the Our Father, Hail Mary and Glory Be into Pame and to write a catechism.

The bronzed Indians, with their straight black hair and dark eyes, joined in as Junipero and Francisco built a beautiful church. The Pames learned from the missionaries how to raise and sell livestock and to grow and harvest crops. But that was not all.

Father Serra, with youthful enthusiasm, made the faith live for his people. He and Francisco taught the children to act out the Christmas story. For Lent, the two friars set up an outdoor Way of the Cross. They led the procession from station to station and the Indians followed silently and devoutly.

During the Holy Thursday Liturgy, Junipero washed the feet of twelve men. The entire village told and retold the event. The faith was coming alive and the priests were overjoyed. But there was still another problem: the adults seemed to believe that frequent confession was not necessary. Father Serra solved the problem. He set up a confessional at the front of the church and went to confession to Father Palou in full view of the awestruck Indians. They were easily won over. If the Padre chose to go to confession, then, who could dare not?

———————

Junipero and Francisco led the Pame tribe to a deep love for Jesus and his Church. Eight years and three months sped by. Two missionaries, again tormented by mosquitos and fleas, trudged back to Mexico City. Other Franciscans would continue their labors in Jalpan.

What did the Lord have in mind for Junipero and Francisco next? Soon they would know. The two men were to spend the next nine years as traveling missionaries. They spent four months a year in Mexico. The rest of the time they visited the people in the eight surrounding dioceses. They celebrated Mass, heard confessions, joined couples in marriage, anointed the seriously ill. Junipero and Francisco loved being priests. They loved the people, too.

CHAPTER 10

A DIFFERENT KIND OF ARMY

A small army of sixteen men in gray robes mounted donkeys. They rode in a caravan over dusty trails for thirty-nine days until they arrived in the city of Tepic, Mexico. This was the first part of a much longer journey.

Junipero was thoughtful. His heart burned for a place he had never seen. He pronounced the word in his mind: *California.* To Father Serra and the missionaries, the image of Baja California meant great numbers of Indians awaiting the good news of Jesus and his Gospel. To the Spanish soldiers accompanying them, Baja California meant wilderness, poverty—the least desirable spot on earth.

At Tepic, the missionaries boarded two ships, the *San Carlos* and the *San Antonio.* The Franciscans hung over the sides of the ships and watched the land slide by. As the ships cut through the waves, the priests' joy mounted. The only gloom on board was in the hearts of the Spanish soldiers and the newly appointed Governor of Baja California, Don Gaspar de Portola.

The Franciscans arrived in lower California.
They touched their sandals on solid ground again.

Junipero walked up to the Governor. The two men stood side by side, hanging on to the ship's railing. The small, round-faced friar with flashing eyes and a set jaw was one kind of Spaniard. He longed for spiritual victories. He dreamed that one day soon a cross would stand on every hill and in every valley of California.

Governor Portola, too, had a determined look, but his goal had nothing to do with religion. He was tall and thin with small, steady eyes and a pointed beard. He looked at his well-groomed nails and smiled a little. Through his head danced visions of wealth and power. His eyes sparkled with the glint of a man whose god is greed.

"I'm not going to like Baja California," Portola said flatly to the priest. "It's hardly what I had in mind." The Governor stared at Junipero. The friar's enthusiasm sickened him.

The *San Carlos* arrived at Loreto, California, four months earlier than the ship, *San Antonio,* on which the rest of the friars rode. Finally, the *San Antonio* arrived and the missionaries made ready for the next part of their journey. On March 14, 1768, the ship, *Concepcion,* slipped out to sea and journeyed two hundred miles to Loreto, the capital of Baja California.

The tired missionaries touched their sandals on solid ground again. The sound of the waves remained in their ears, and their bodies still felt the rocking of the ships. Junipero looked around at the barren outpost. It was nothing more than a few adobe huts on the edge of the frontier. The priest chuckled.

"If this is the capital," he said to himself, "imagine what the rest of Baja is like."

Fifteen missions had already been started in lower California, but they were far from flourishing. When the Franciscans arrived to take over the missions, Father Serra had become the president or director of the mission cluster. He appointed a friar to be in charge of each one.

"Francisco," Father Serra said to Palou, "you shall have *San Javier*." In his imagination, Junipero could picture the fiery Jesuit missionary, Saint Francis Xavier, the patron of that mission. Francisco Palou would no doubt match him in zeal and courage, he thought.

"Father Crespi," Junipero continued, "you will have *La Purisima*, named after Mary, the pure one, because of your special love for the Mother of God.

"Father Lasuen, you will have *San Borja*, named after the great bishop of Geneva, Switzerland, Saint Francis Borgia.

"Father Parron, you and I will take Mission *Loreto*, which honors Mary as Our Lady of Loreto."

The great expedition was begun.

CHAPTER 11

SPARKS AND FLAMES

It was Easter morning, 1769. After he celebrated Mass, Junipero and a few companions left Mission Loreto and arrived at Mission San Javier by evening. Serra was determined to travel by foot or mule to every mission in Baja, then on to Upper California. His friend, Palou, was overjoyed to see him but was quick to notice Junipero's swollen leg.

"Be realistic, Junipero," Father Palou argued, "you can barely walk. How can you speak of founding missions, of conquering new territories, in that condition? I should go instead. Yes, let me go."

"That is out of the question," replied Junipero. "I have put my trust in God and he will help me."

Father Serra stayed at San Javier three days and then prepared to continue his journey. Francisco tried again to stop him, but he knew it would be useless. Junipero wanted to lighten the atmosphere. After he had mounted his mule, he turned to Father Palou and exclaimed, "To our meeting in

Monterey, where we shall soon find ourselves working together again!"

At this, Francisco, fearing that Junipero would die during the journey, broke down and sobbed, "No, no...to our meeting in eternity."

"It hurts me when you speak like that," Junipero scolded. "You lack faith." Then he smiled kindly at Father Palou and started his mule down the rocky path. Always forward, never back.

Junipero moved steadily up the peninsula of Baja California. He passed the missions of San Jose, La Purisima, San Ignacio, Santa Gertrudis and finally San Borja where he spent two days with Father Lasuen. On May 13, he reached Velicato, where he was greeted by the soldiers who had arrived before him.

The next day, Pentecost Sunday, Junipero celebrated Mass for the Indians. He was overjoyed at the fervor of the men, women and children. The pages of his memory turned back. He was a novice in Palma, Spain, again where the sparks of missionary zeal had become a flame. Then his memory returned to the present. Here he was in California. The priest looked at the Indians, then up to the sky. Somehow he felt that Francis Solano would be proud of him.

As Junipero pulled the rough blanket over his bed of boards that night, he sighed happily.

Dawn broke and gilded the landscape with its rays. Junipero had already gotten up. He knelt, praying on the earthen floor of his cabin. He got up and answered a knock at the door. It was a man who brought news that a group of Indians was waiting to see him. Father Serra was jubilant. He bent low to kiss the bare soil beneath his feet.

"At last! At last!" he exclaimed. "The hour has come when I will see those who have been ignorant of Christ and who from now on will be my friends."

As he emerged from the cabin, a band of twelve Indians met his gaze, standing with Father Campa, the priest who would be staying at the mission.

Junipero greeted them and smiled broadly. Motioning to Father Campa he said to the Indians, "Come to see him often. He will be your best friend."

The Indians liked the priests and promised to be friendly. It had been a good beginning.

The friar smiled kindly as the muleteer applied the crude
medicine to his leg.

CHAPTER 12

A BOY AND A CURE

Junipero continued his journey up the California coast. The friar, however, was growing worried. The old leg infection which he had developed on the way to Mexico City was active once more. On May 17, he wrote in his diary:

"Shall I have to follow the expedition on a stretcher? I can no longer stand upright: my leg, from which I have suffered so much during the past year, is now swollen to the knee."

How could he ever hope to conquer the long miles of walking ahead of him? When the friars and Indians urged him not to continue, he responded, "Even if I die here on the trail, I will not go back. You may bury me here and I shall very gladly remain among these pagan people, if such be the will of God."

Lying on a cot, with pain searing his leg, Father Serra asked that the boy who cared for the mules come to his cabin.

"Juan! Juan Coronel! Welcome!" The young muleteer stepped shyly inside the cabin.

"Juan, would you have some way of curing me?"

At these words, the boy's face twisted in confusion.

"Father," he exclaimed, "I'm not a physician. I only cure animals!"

"I see," the priest said, as he smiled weakly. "I will be your 'animal,' Juan. Pretend that I am one of your sick mules and cure me."

The boy stood looking at the priest. Slowly a question formed on his lips, "Are you sure, Father?"

Junipero nodded his head. Juan began to tremble. "Maybe we can bring you outside under the big tree, Father. I'll get my supplies." With that, Juan was off.

Junipero settled himself under a large oak and waited patiently. In minutes the boy was back. He brought animal fat and herbs which he mixed and heated.

"I'm sorry, Father. It doesn't look too nice, but I hope it will work."

The friar smiled kindly as the crude medicine was applied to his leg. "That's fine, son. The important thing is that I can walk again. There is so much good still to do."

After the treatment was finished, the boy left and Father Serra remained outside a little longer.

The day was beautiful and he was sure that God would heal his leg. That night the priest slept soundly, and awoke the next morning ready to mount the saddle. To those who were astonished by the sudden improvement, Junipero replied, "When the Lord wants something, he accomplishes it."

Junipero left Baja and was now in Upper California.
He gazed at the beautiful port of San Diego.

CHAPTER 13

TO BEAUTIFUL SAN DIEGO

Junipero left Baja and was now in Upper California. As he and his traveling companions—Governor Portola included—moved north, the desert was replaced by grassy hills and grapevines. The fresh, green earth reminded Father Serra of Majorca. The group plodded on toward the bay of San Diego. Someone spotted it and shouted. They had reached their destination.

Father Serra gazed at the beautiful port of San Diego. His eyes penetrated the water as his thoughts raced. His journeys by ship, by mule and on foot had taken him far from his homeland. He wanted to plant the cross of Jesus in this beautiful land. Junipero thought about the friendly Indians who had waited along the paths and trails to welcome the strangers. If only he could have known that before his death he would baptize six thousand, seven hundred and thirty-six Indians.

The ships *San Antonio* and *San Carlos* had arrived, but there was trouble. The *San Carlos*, driven off course by a storm, had arrived six weeks late. Scurvy, the dreaded disease of seamen, tor-

mented the crew. All but two sailors had con-
tracted it and were dead or dying.

Father Serra and Governor Portola found that
the camp had been turned into a frontier hospital.
It was decided that the *San Antonio* should return
with a small crew to San Blas in Baja California,
part of present-day Mexico, to bring back supplies
and more men. Father Serra would stay at San
Diego to begin the new mission. All other Spaniards well enough to make the trip would travel
north by land, under Governor Portola and Father
Juan Crespi, to find Monterey Harbor.

Mission San Diego officially began on the
morning of July 16, 1769. It was a warm day.
Bright blue waves rolled over the sand of the
nearby beach. Spanish soldiers planted a wooden
cross atop a hill, later to be called Presidio Hill.
Fray Junipero blessed the cross and celebrated
Mass.

A large bell, hoisted to the branch of a tree,
was rung, loud and long. Its joyful tones penetrated the wilderness, inviting the Indians to come
to the Mission. The Indians must have wondered
what the loud clanging meant. Not one of them
appeared all day.

"That's all right," Junipero chuckled to himself. "We probably startled them. They will come
to see us soon enough, even if for nothing other
than curiosity."

Father Serra stood alone now on the hill.
Twilight was giving way to a dark, starry night, and

the sun had long before dipped into the waters of the bay. Everything was still, and crickets added their chirping to the quiet sounds of evening.

Junipero sat down beneath a large tree. Slowly, he breathed in the cool night air. His thoughts drifted again back through the years, and across the ocean to his novitiate days. He had been thinking about that more and more lately. What an ambitious dream it had been to become a missionary in the New World. As he felt the cool earth beneath his tired body, the priest realized that so far he had traveled eight thousand miles from home.

Now, at the age of fifty-six, Junipero was in Upper California and somehow he knew that he would spend the rest of his life here.

"As long as life lasts in me," Junipero said, "I shall do all I can to propagate our holy faith. In California is my way of life and, please God, here I hope to die."

CHAPTER 14

SILENCE BEFORE THE STORM

"We must begin at once," Father Serra said thoughtfully. "What good followers of Jesus our San Diego Indians will make."

The Indians came closer and closer to the mission. They began to smile and attempted to talk to Father Serra and the others. Intelligent and good-natured, both men and women wore paint on their faces and seashells on their noses and ears. They lived in small huts made of brush and reeds.

Junipero loved the people with a true missionary's heart.

"A harvest of souls can be gathered into the Church without too much difficulty," he said with a smile. But in spite of the priest's obvious affection for them, some of the Indians began to steal from the camp. On the morning of a warm August day, one of the other Franciscans, Father Parron, boarded the San Carlos to celebrate Mass for the sailors. Only Father Serra and Father Vizcaino were left at the mission.

Everything was quiet, with an occasional rustling in the trees as a breeze blew through the leaves. Even the birds were silent. Suddenly, sharp cries split the stillness, followed by the shouts of terrified Spaniards in the make-shift hospital.

"Indian attack! Indian attack!" someone shouted. He was right. Indians in war paint began ripping sheets and shirts from the patients. Able-bodied soldiers hastily pulled on their leather jackets and rushed to the scene. Now the war cries were matched by the booming of Spanish muskets.

Father Serra heard a soft moan. Jose-Maria, an Indian youth, newly baptized, fell into the room. He had been pierced through the throat by an arrow.

"Father, forgive my sins," Jose cried. "I am going to die." The priest ran to the boy and picked him up. He held him in his arms and tried to ease the pain and fright.

"Don't be afraid, Jose," Junipero whispered. "In a little while, you will be with Jesus. You will go to heaven where there is no pain or sadness."

Jose smiled weakly and closed his eyes. The priest held the boy in his arms for a long time and then he knew that Jose had gone to God. He laid the child gently on the floor, and knelt beside him.

Finally, the fighting died down. The Indians retreated with their dead and wounded and there was a sad kind of quiet. The only Christian to die in the fight was Jose. Three others had been wounded by arrows.

It was a painful thing for Junipero to see how some of his beloved Indians repaid his goodness.

"Ah, well," he sighed, "they are not yet Christian. They don't know any better. If only they had asked for what they wanted.... We would have gladly given it to them."

Although the soldiers were now angry with the Indians, the Franciscan priests loved them as much as ever. Father Serra prayed and waited for the return of his wayward children. And return they did.

A few days later, Indians, wounded by soldiers' bullets, came limping into the camp. They asked to be cured by the physician, Doctor Prat. Father Serra turned to the bewildered doctor and with a smile, said, "Please, help my children. Christian charity requires this of us."

Soon the renegades were coming regularly to the mission again. Junipero was overjoyed. The kind-hearted friar could never have imagined the suffering that still lay ahead for Mission San Diego.

CHAPTER 15

WHITE SAIL ON THE SEA

Explorers, led by Governor Portola, had found San Francisco Bay. They had camped near what would one day be Los Angeles, but had missed the Bay of Monterey. The exhausted men returned to Mission San Diego.

"You didn't find it? How can that be?" Junipero asked.

"I'm telling you, Father," Portola said weakly, "the Bay of Monterey was either the figment of someone's imagination or has since disappeared. We journeyed over seven hundred miles north and found nothing of this legendary place. As you can see by looking at us, we barely made it back alive. On our return journey, we were forced to kill our own mules for food."

Junipero patted the exasperated Governor on the shoulder.

"Don't be discouraged," the priest said kindly. "Just be patient. God wills this work and he will show us the way."

"Patience...patience," Portola grumbled. "It is already the end of January. How long can we live on patience?" He left the room still mumbling.

The days of February ticked off the calendar and March began. Mission San Diego had been reduced to a pitiful condition. A messenger had arrived with the grim news that the supply ship, San Jose, which had been expected from Baja, had been lost at sea. Governor Portola and his seventy-three soldiers were frustrated. Starvation lurked. Supplies were desperately needed now.

Father Serra spent more time than ever on his knees.

"Heavenly Father, Creator of all that is, remember us here at your mission. If we are forced to leave because of lack of food, how will our beloved Indians learn to know and love you? If the soldiers leave, how can we poor friars stay on here?"

The priest bowed his head and remained silent for a long time. When he stood up, he had an idea. It was as clear as the San Diego sky that day.

Who had provided for Jesus and Mary while they lived on earth? Saint Joseph, of course. And whose feast day would be celebrated soon, on March 19? Saint Joseph's, of course. Father Serra's face lit with joy as he knocked on Governor Portola's door.

"Yes?" the Governor asked curtly. "Come in."

"Governor, I invite you to join me in an act of faith," the priest said graciously.

"How?" asked Portola.

A speck of white dotted the horizon. The speck grew larger until it formed a sail. "A supply ship!" someone shouted.

"Nine days before Saint Joseph's feast, let us begin prayers in his honor, begging his help for our mission here."

Portola scratched his head. "Why, I haven't made a *novena* to a saint since I was a boy," he mumbled. "But things are so bad, Padre, that I'm willing to revive an old custom."

Day after day, the priest, the Governor and others at the mission recited their prayers to Saint Joseph. Day after day, no supplies arrived. The novena to Saint Joseph ended. The morning of the great saint's feast had arrived. Junipero celebrated Mass and preached a glowing homily on Saint Joseph's great love for Jesus and Mary.

After a meager breakfast, the soldiers began to pack for departure. Father Serra was in agony, fearing that Upper California would be abandoned.

March 19 dragged on. Junipero spent hours in prayer. At three o'clock in the afternoon, a speck of white dotted the horizon. The speck grew larger until it formed a sail.

"A supply ship!" someone shouted. The entire camp strained their eyes to see. It was true! It was really true! Father Serra had already fallen to his knees, wrapped in thankful prayer to Saint Joseph. The rest of the camp followed his example.

CHAPTER 16

THE MARVEL OF MONTEREY

Governor Portola and Father Crespi led an overland expedition north. After turning Mission San Diego over to Fathers Parron and Gomez, Junipero sailed from San Diego harbor on the *San Antonio*. Whether walking or sailing, the men had one destination: Monterey Bay.

The Governor and his companions found the missing bay. Waves lapped the shore and the blue ocean blended into the horizon. The smooth blanket of sand on the beach was bleached by the warm sun. The beauty of Monterey Bay was no secret to the Indians, who although not visible, were there. But while the Indians stayed out of sight, hundreds of seals and otters splashed in the ocean and laid on the sandy beach, soaking in the warm sun.

"I wouldn't have believed that any place in the world could be more beautiful than San Diego harbor," one of the soldiers said. "But look at this.... Just look." The Spaniards stared in awe. Monterey Bay was breathtaking.

While the explorers awaited the arrival of the *San Antonio,* they walked over the hills to *Point Pinos.* Ten months earlier, the same men had planted a wooden cross on that hill. It was still there. At the base, feathers and broken arrows had been stuck in the ground. The Spaniards cheered when they saw those symbols of friendship left by the Indians whose land it was. Governor Portola and Father Crespi went near the cross. They saw other gifts, too, such as fresh meat and sardines.

The men looked quickly around, but the Indians could not be seen. Still, the *San Antonio* did not arrive. While they waited, Governor Portola, Father Crespi and a guard decided to explore Carmel Bay. Friendly Indians came with gifts. Seeing the Spaniards' joy, the Indians returned with more meat and seeds for planting.

Seven days passed by. Finally, the *San Antonio,* with Father Serra among its passengers, sailed into view. On a Monterey hilltop, Governor Portola lit three large bonfires. These had been the signal which Portola and Captain Perez of the *San Antonio* had agreed upon. The Captain saw the signal and responded with cannon fire.

Junipero touched his sandals on Monterey. It was June 1, 1770. The new Mission, San Carlos, would be started two days later, on Pentecost Sunday. The great feast of Corpus Christi was just a week and a half away.

"Let us celebrate this feast of the Body and Blood of Jesus with as much solemnity as we can,"

Father Serra said to the men in the camp. They glanced at each other, question marks written all over their faces. Where would they get church supplies to make a fitting celebration?

"Search the ship and take what you can use," Perez told his men. "And remember, Father Serra wants candles, lots of candles, for a procession."

"Candles?" one of the sailors asked. "But, sir, I hardly think we will find procession candles."

"If you don't," Perez said with a smile playing on the edges of his mouth, "you'll be the one to tell Father Serra."

While a group of sailors turned a new storage house into a temporary chapel, others hung banners of saints and set up the silver missal stand and candlesticks brought from Loreto. Green branches were cut and placed on the path along which the procession would pass.

The sailors who searched the ship were shocked to find two boxes of procession candles. Everyone was surprised except a little friar with a pronounced limp.

The feast of Corpus Christi was celebrated in splendor at Mission San Carlos. The soldiers rang bells and the sailors shot cannon balls to salute their Lord present in the Blessed Sacrament.

It was a glorious day for Junipero Serra.

CHAPTER 17

THE GOLDEN CHAIN

The San Carlos Mission at Monterey was in the hands of forty men, including the friars and Baja Indians. Five hundred miles away Mission San Diego had only twenty-three people. The new guardian of San Fernando Mission in Lower California was Father Rafael Verger. He, like Fathers Serra and Palou, was an ex-professor from Majorca.

Junipero sighed and thanked God for Father Verger...an excellent choice. He would take good care of the Baja Indians and protect them from injustice.

Meanwhile, the prayers and penances of Junipero and the friars at San Carlos were being answered. The day after Christmas, 1770, Father Serra baptized a five-year-old Indian boy, Bernardino de Jesus. By the following May, 1771, twenty more Indians had been baptized.

On May 21, 1771, Captain Perez sailed the *San Antonio* into Monterey Bay. Nine new friar-missionaries had arrived.

The ship also brought a letter from Viceroy Bucareli in Mexico. Mission San Carlos, he said, could be moved to the banks of the Carmel River, a much better location for evangelizing the Indians. The friars also had his permission to begin five new missions between Monterey and San Diego.

Father Serra was overjoyed. In his imagination, he saw a golden chain of missions. Soon, with God's help, all the California Indians would hear the Good News of Christianity.

The disappointing part of the Viceroy's letter was the appointment of Commandante Pedro Fages as the representative of the government to whom the friars would be responsible.

Ambitious and unbending, Fages seemed annoyed by the friars, and most especially by Father Serra. But the friar was not to be frightened by him. Eventually, the friction caused by the ambition of Fages and the apostolic zeal of Serra reached its peak.

Junipero journeyed to Mexico City to plead his case on behalf of the struggling California missions. Guardian Verger, his Franciscan superior, and Viceroy Bucareli, representing the Spanish government, came to Serra's aid.

All the while, the golden chain was growing. Mission San Antonio de Padua began on July 14, 1771; Mission San Gabriel Archangel, September 8, 1771; Mission San Luis Obispo, September 1, 1772; Mission San Francisco de Asis, October 9, 1776; Mission San Juan Capistrano, November 1, 1776; Mission Santa Clara de Asis, January 12,

1777. Father Serra's last would be Mission San Buenaventura, to be founded on March 31, 1782.

Of all the missions in Upper California, the first one—Mission San Diego—was to cause the most suffering to Junipero and the friars.

In 1775, the troubled mission was to receive another Indian attack.

CHAPTER 18

WAR CRIES

The night was starless and dark. A chill ran through Father Vicente Fuster as he walked from the kitchen to his room. It was too quiet.

"Father Jayme and the others are probably already asleep and here I am worrying," the priest thought to himself. His imagination painted pictures of Monterey Mission and Father Serra. He wished he could be with Father Serra at least for a few days.

"Mission San Diego is still your first mission in Upper California, Junipero. How I wish you were here now," the priest whispered.

Carlos, a renegade Christian Indian chief, knew that there were only seventy soldiers protecting the California missions along the five hundred mile coastal strip. The chief had convinced himself and a few others that the gray-robed friars, Father Fuster and Father Jayme, of the San Diego Mission, were enemies of the Indians.

Carlos had gone from village to village and won over six hundred braves to his cause. Now he led them silently through the woods. The men

Six hundred braves surrounded Mission San Diego.
War cries—loud and terrible—filled the air.

surrounded Mission San Diego. Their eyes glowed with hate. They would destroy these enemies once and for all.

Two friars, a carpenter, a blacksmith, a handful of soldiers and a group of devout Indians who were spending the night at the mission to assist at Mass the next morning—they were the enemies.

War cries—loud and terrible—pierced the air. Small fires sprung up and soon raged into large fires. The Indians shot arrows and hurled mud at the adobe buildings. The warriors surrounded the huts of the Christian Indians and threatened them with death if they tried to help the Padres. The Church was looted. By this time the warriors were afraid of no one and nothing.

At the height of the nightmare, gentle Father Jayme walked outside into the courtyard. He raised his arms high, as Saint Francis himself would have done, and greeted his converts.

"Love God, my children," the young priest said. This was his usual greeting to the Indians whom he loved so much. He had heard rumors of possible attacks, but he had refused to believe such things of his "children."

Carlos and four other Indians pumped the priest's body with arrows. As he fell in a pool of his own blood, he formed the words slowly but distinctly, "Love God, my children...."

The Indians dragged the priest to a stream and pelted his face and body with rocks.

Christians from neighboring Indian villages heard the war cries and saw the fires. They came to help the friars ward off the attack. But still the arrows rained all through the night. The little group at the mission was desperately outnumbered. The soldiers put down their muskets and knelt with Father Fuster and prayed, "Mother of God...help us. Spare us."

Father Fuster stood up and looked around the dark room for Father Luis Jayme. He wrenched his hands and said a prayer. The priest ran to check Father Luis' bed. It was empty. Fuster moved cautiously around the mission compound, dodging arrows. He kept a cushion near his face and neck, as he lunged from one building to another. An arrow pierced the cushion clear through and stopped just short of his neck. He had looked everywhere possible. Still Father Jayme could not be found.

At last, the dawn brought the first streaks of light. The arrows stopped and silence resumed as if never interrupted. But the nightmare was not over.

"Father Luis!" Fuster called. He walked out into the courtyard and along the road, shouting for Father Jayme. He was terrified now. Christian Indians ran up to the haggard priest and tried to comfort him.

But no, they said sorrowfully, they did not know where the other priest was. More and more friendly Indians from the neighboring villages came to assure Father Fuster that he and the mission would have their protection. He was grateful, but still, where was Father Jayme?

Indian women approached him timidly, and led him to the creek on the outskirts of the mission. Every bit of strength drained from Fuster as he beheld the battered body of his friend. He staggered, and the Indians caught him as he fainted.

When Father Fuster revived, he led the sorrowful procession accompanying the body of his thirty-five year old companion, Father Luis Jayme, four miles back to the camp. Father Jayme and Jose Romero, the blacksmith, were buried on November 6 with Urcelino, the carpenter, who had died a few days after being wounded.

More than a month later, messengers arrived at Monterey and informed Father Serra of the massacre. It was December 13. The priest lowered his head, and in a hoarse voice whispered, "Now that San Diego has been bathed in blood, the Indians will be converted. The blood of martyrs," he said, "is the seed of the Church."

Carlos, the renegade, turned himself in. He was imprisoned by the authorities. At the missionaries' request, he was freed, unharmed, and returned to the Padres.

Father Serra journeyed to San Diego. Of the five Indians who had killed Father Jayme, three had been Christians. They repented. During his stay in San Diego, Father Serra administered the

Sacrament of Confirmation to them. Of the two non-Christians, one died after becoming a Christian; the other disappeared.

Father Serra led the group of priests, Indians, sailors and soldiers who made seven thousand adobe bricks and rebuilt the mission. Everyone participated willingly. A spirit of joy and love rebuilt Mission San Diego. Perhaps that was the gift of a young friar who had paid for the mission with his life. Echoes of Father Jayme's voice seemed to fill the air: "Love God, my children."

CHAPTER 19

MEMORIES

Father Serra rubbed his leg to ease the throbbing. The chest pains were becoming more frequent, too. During part of 1783 until July, 1784, the priest made a final tour of the missions in Upper California. As he and his companions rode by mule down trails bordered by lush trees and playful animals, the aging priest prayed. The faces of his Indian converts lived in his memory. They had been worth every painful step and every sleepless night.

"The greatest sacrifice," he said to himself, "was the cruel death of gentle Father Jayme. That almost killed me, Jayme, but now you have your gray-robed companions up there with you...good Father Crespi and Father Murguia. We miss all three of you, Jayme."

A tear slipped down Serra's face as he pushed ahead on the trail.

"I will be with you soon, my sons," he continued. "Wait for me. Wait for me."

Junipero arrived back at Mission San Carlos. It seemed as if the priest had caught a glimpse of

the future. He knew that Brother Death—as Saint
Francis of Assisi would say—was just around the
corner. Father Serra became more quiet than
usual. He spent hours praying. Then walking
through Mission San Carlos, he smiled at his beloved Indians and blessed each one.

One day the priest picked up his feather pen
and dipped it into the ink bottle. He wrote to the
missions asking that a representative from each be
sent to San Carlos.

"I want to give the friars one of my personal
possessions as a memento of my friendship," he
said.

The sun shown in a cloudless Monterey sky. It
was August 18. Father Serra propped himself up
on a small wooden bench outside the mission
church. A mule plodded closer and closer. Junipero's tired eyes strained to see the face of the
rider. The Franciscan friar on the mule recognized
him first. Francisco Palou slid from his mount and
ran toward the priest. He embraced Father Serra,
then took a step back, while still holding his friend
firmly by the shoulders.

Palou was speechless. Junipero was so ill that
he could barely hold his head up. Yet, with Father
Francisco once again at his side, he rallied.

"My son," Junipero said gratefully, "I've
waited for you to come. I would like to make a
general confession of my whole life to you."

"Certainly, my Father," Francisco stammered.
The two priests walked slowly into the church.

"My son," Junipero said to Francisco, "I would like
to make a general confession of my whole life to you."

Father Serra smiled, bent his head in silence for a long while, then began: "Bless me, Father, for I have sinned. This is a general confession of the sins of my whole life."

Junipero confessed his sins and received Jesus' forgiveness through the words pronounced by beloved Palou. Then, the priests sat for a long while on the small bench outside. Junipero whispered his fears that the Franciscans might be expelled by Spanish authorities from Upper and Lower California.

"With your prayers, good Father," Palou said kindly, "the Franciscans will never lose California."

CHAPTER 20

BEYOND *EL CAMINO REAL*

Father Serra sat in the mission chapel. He was surrounded by convert Indians. Father Palou celebrated the Mass and Junipero prayed quietly. The priest moved his head to see the Indians, crowded on every bench, following the Mass and singing joyfully. After Mass, Father Serra looked up and smiled. The Indians clustered around the gentle man and knelt to receive his blessing.

The August days passed. The night of August 25 was painful for Junipero. The morning of August 26, the mission carpenter hurried to Father Palou.

"Father," he said anxiously, "Father Serra has asked me to do something I don't want to do.... In fact, it is something I can't do. I *won't* do."

Francisco had never seen the carpenter so upset. The priest frowned and asked, "What is it?"

"To start making his coffin," the man whispered. Father Palou winced, then patted the man gently on the shoulder.

"Do as he says," Francisco replied.

August 26 passed into August 27. Father Palou and a circle of Indians clustered around Junipero. His face was pale. His once lively features seemed waxen. It was as though his life and strength were being squeezed from him drop by drop.

"I am dying, Francisco," the priest said softly. "I want to receive my Lord in Holy Communion for the last time."

"I will bring the Sacred Host to you, Father," Palou said gently.

"Oh, no," Father Serra exclaimed. "I insist on going to the chapel to receive my God." Francisco helped the priest to stand up. Junipero felt the sharp pains in his leg and leaned heavily on his friend. Together they began to walk the hundred yards to the church.

Beads of perspiration formed on Palou's forehead and tears filled his eyes.

"My father," Francisco pleaded, "this is too much for you. Let me bring the Lord here."

Father Serra shook his head firmly. He smiled and whispered, "It is no trouble to go to chapel, Francisco. Thank you for helping me."

It was 10:00 on the morning of August 28, the Feast of Saint Augustine. The officers of the ship, *San Carlos*, arrived with a priest from Lima, Peru, whom Father Serra knew. Junipero asked that the mission bells be rung to honor the visitors.

Around noon, Junipero and Francisco sat on the bench outside and talked.

"Francisco," Serra said suddenly, "I want you to bury me in the church near Father Crespi for now. When the stone church is built, put me wherever you wish."

Father Palou felt his world unraveling and his eyes filled with tears. He mumbled something about getting a cup of broth for the priest and hurried off. A few minutes later he returned and handed the cup to Junipero. The sick priest took it and smiled, then sipped the hot broth slowly. He set the cup down and said, "Now I would like to rest."

Leaning on Father Palou, he walked slowly to his room. Father Serra stretched out on the boards that were his bed and covered himself with a blanket. He clutched his crucifix tightly and crossed his hands over his chest. The priest's body relaxed and his eyes closed. Father Palou slipped out of the room and shut the door softly. A few hours later, a strange feeling crept over Francisco. He trembled slightly and hurried to Junipero's room. He opened the door slowly and saw that his friend was resting in the same position he had left him nearly three hours before. Palou stood silently at the foot of the bed and watched to see if Junipero was breathing. But the figure on the bed was still.

Tears streamed down Francisco's face. He crept closer and stared into the peaceful face.

"Junipero," he whispered, "Junipero." He gazed one long last moment at the small man with a heart of fire.

"Wait for me, Junipero," Palou said, as the tears continued to flow. "Wait for me."

Father Palou asked a few Indians to ring the Church bells announcing Junipero's death. People streamed into the Mission. Many of the Indians wept. The friars gathered. They slipped the sandals from the dead man's feet and placed him in the open coffin prepared by the village carpenter.

A sorrowful procession filed in and out of Father Serra's room. Indians and soldiers, sailors and colonists walked up to the still body. Some placed wreaths of wild flowers around his neck. Others touched rosaries and medals to his face.

In the evening, Father Serra's body was moved to the church. All through the night, groups surrounded the silent missionary and prayed for his soul.

As dawn turned the horizon into a stunning red glow, the crowd gathered for the funeral. All six hundred Indian converts living at San Carlos Mission, the soldiers and guards and the crew of the *San Carlos* squeezed into the church and sang a Mass for the dead.

Throughout the day, the body remained in the church. An endless stream of people filed by. At half-hour intervals throughout the day cannons were fired in salute.

In the late afternoon, the large crowd gathered in procession. The cross bearer and altar boys were in the lead, followed by the Indians, soldiers and sailors.

Last were the friars. Then Father Palou. The procession wound around the courtyard and into the Church sanctuary. Father Serra's coffin was lowered next to the coffin of Father Crespi. The friars stood silently, staring at the stark scene.

"Farewell, Junipero." Father Palou whispered. "Farewell for now. Remember...wait for me."

Father Palou left the church and walked silently to Junipero's room. He looked around the small, bare cell. Suddenly, he remembered the dead priest's sandals which he had given away that afternoon as keepsakes. Father Serra's worn, leather sandals—what a story of dedication they could tell. He smiled to himself and asked softly, "How many friars will it take to fill your shoes, Junipero?"

ST. PAUL BOOK & MEDIA CENTERS
OPERATED BY THE DAUGHTERS OF ST. PAUL

ALASKA
750 West 5th Ave., Anchorage, AK 99501 **907-272-8183.**
CALIFORNIA
3908 Sepulveda Blvd., Culver City, CA 90230 **213-202-8144.**
1570 Fifth Ave. (at Cedar Street), San Diego, CA 92101 **619-232-1442.**
46 Geary Street, San Francisco, CA 94108 **415-781-5180.**
FLORIDA
Coral Park Shopping Center, 9808 S.W. 8 St., Miami, FL 33174
305-559-6715; 305-559-6716.
HAWAII
1143 Bishop Street, Honolulu, HI 96813 **808-521-2731.**
ILLINOIS
172 North Michigan Ave., Chicago, IL 60601 **312-346-4228; 312-346-3240.**
LOUISIANA
423 Main Street, Baton Rouge, LA 70802 **504-343-4057; 504-336-1504.**
4403 Veterans Memorial Blvd., Metairie, LA 70006 **504-887-7631;**
504-887-0113.
MASSACHUSETTS
50 St. Paul's Ave., Jamaica Plain, Boston, MA 02130 **617-522-8911.**
Rte. 1, 450 Providence Hwy., Dedham, MA 02026 **617-326-5385.**
MISSOURI
1001 Pine Street (at North 10th), St. Louis, MO 63101 **314-621-0346.**
NEW JERSEY
Hudson Mall, Route 440 and Communipaw Ave.,
Jersey City, NJ 07304 **201-433-7740.**
NEW YORK
625 East 187th Street, Bronx, NY 10458 **212-584-0440.**
59 East 43rd Street, New York, NY 10017 **212-986-7580.**
78 Fort Place, Staten Island, NY 10301 **718-447-5071; 718-447-5086.**
OHIO
616 Walnut Street, Cincinnati, OH 45202 **513-421-5733.**
2105 Ontario Street (at Prospect Ave.), Cleveland, OH 44115
216-621-9427.
PENNSYLVANIA
1719 Chestnut Street, Philadelphia, PA 19103 **215-568-2638;**
215-864-0991.
SOUTH CAROLINA
243 King Street, Charleston, SC 29401 **803-577-0175.**
TEXAS
114 Main Plaza, San Antonio, TX 78205 **512-224-8101.**
VIRGINIA
1025 King Street, Alexandria, VA 22314 **703-549-3806.**
WASHINGTON
2301 Second Ave. (at Bell), Seattle, WA 98121 **206-441-4100.**
CANADA
3022 Dufferin Street, Toronto 395, Ontario, Canada.